The Daily Czech Challenge

Learn 10 Czech Words a Day for 7 Weeks

Introduction ✹

Welcome 🙌 to "Learn 10 Czech Words a Day for 7 Weeks"! This guide ✊ is crafted to offer a fun 🎉 and effective way for kids and beginners to dive into the Czech language. With a mix of carefully picked words and interactive methods, we aim to turn language learning into an enjoyable adventure 🚀.

Embarking on the journey of a new language can be thrilling and a bit daunting ⬤, but no worries! We've designed this book 📖 with your learning journey in mind. Every day, you'll discover ten Czech words, chosen for their usefulness in everyday life 🍂. These words span various themes, helping you grow your vocabulary and boost your confidence in speaking and understanding.

To help you learn, we've paired each Czech word with its English counterpart ▄▆▄, making it easier to draw connections between the two languages. Practice writing the Czech words four times each to strengthen your memory and build a solid base in the language. Enjoy the thrill of uncovering new words daily, gradually enhancing your skills step by step 🧍.

Consider this book your seven-week learning buddy ■, guiding you with a structured approach. Each week introduces fresh vocabulary while reinforcing what you've already learned, ensuring you consolidate your knowledge. Dedicate a few minutes daily to the exercises and activities ■. Remember, consistency is key 🔑, and your effort will be greatly rewarded.

Whether you're a young language lover or a beginner eager to learn, this book caters to you ●. The lively illustrations and interactive tasks aim to ignite your imagination and keep you motivated. Remember, learning a language is about having fun 🎈, and we hope this book lights up your passion for Czech.

As you start this language learning journey, embrace the challenge, celebrate your milestones 🎉, and enjoy every moment. Learning 10 Czech words a day is a reachable goal, and with commitment and enthusiasm, you're on your way to opening new doors of communication and insight 🔑.

Happy learning! 🎓

Attention: The provided English pronunciations of the Czech words are approximations. The actual pronunciation may vary depending on regional accents and dialects in the Czech Republic. Furthermore, some Czech sounds cannot be precisely reproduced in English, meaning that the pronunciations can slightly deviate from the original Czech sounds.

Table of Contents

Week 1

Day 1: Numbers

One	Jeden (YEH-dehn)
Two	Dva (dvah)
Three	Tři (trzhee)
Four	Čtyři (ch-TIR-zhee)
Five	Pět (pyet)
Six	Šest (shehst)
Seven	Sedm (sehd-m)
Eight	Osm (ohsm)
Nine	Devět (DEH-vyet)
Ten	Deset (DEH-seht)

Write the right words down twice on the next page

Six	....	....
Two	....	....
Eight	....	....
Four	....	....
Five	....	....
Eight	....	....
Seven	....	....
Three	....	....
Nine	....	....
Ten	....	....
One	....	....
Two	....	....
Ten	....	....
Four	....	....
Five	....	....
Six	....	....
Seven	....	....
Three	....	....
Nine	....	....
One	....	....

Week 1

Day 2: Colors

Red	Červená (CHER-veh-nah)
Blue	Modrá (MOHD-rah)
Yellow	Žlutá (ZHLOO-tah)
Green	Zelená (ZEHL-eh-nah)
Orange	Oranžová (oh-RAHN-zhoh-vah)
Purple	Fialová (FEE-ah-loh-vah)
Pink	Růžová (ROO-zhoh-vah)
Black	Černá (CHER-nah)
White	Bílá (BEE-lah)
Gray	Šedá (SHEH-dah)

Write the right words down twice on the next page

Red	....	....
Purple	....	....
White	....	....
Gray	....	....
Orange	....	....
Purple	....	....
Blue	....	....
Black	....	....
White	....	....
Gray	....	....
Pink	....	....
Blue	....	....
Yellow	....	....
Green	....	....
Orange	....	....
Pink	....	....
Red	....	....
Black	....	....
Yellow	....	....
Green	....	....

Week 1

Day 3: Family

Mother	Matka (MAHT-kah)
Father	Otec (OH-tehts)
Brother	Bratr (BRAH-tr)
Sister	Sestra (SEHS-trah)
Son	Syn (seen)
Daughter	Dcera (DTSER-ah)
Grandfather	Dědeček (DYEH-deh-chek)
Grandmother	Babička (BAH-bee-chkah)
Uncle	Strýc (STREETS)
Aunt	Teta (TEH-tah)

Write the right words down twice on the next page

Aunt	....	....
Father	....	....
Mother	....	....
Uncle	....	....
Brother	....	....
Sister	....	....
Son	....	....
Daughter	....	....
Grandfather	....	....
Sister	....	....
Aunt	....	....
Grandmother	....	....
Uncle	....	....
Son	....	....
Grandmother	....	....
Father	....	....
Brother	....	....
Daughter	....	....
Grandfather	....	....
Mother	....	....

Week 1

Day 4: Food

Bread	Chléb (khlehb)
Rice	Rýže (REE-zheh)
Meat	Maso (MAH-soh)
Vegetables	Zelenina (ZEHL-eh-nee-nah)
Fruit	Ovoce (OH-voh-tseh)
Milk	Mléko (MLEH-koh)
Cheese	Sýr (seer)
Eggs	Vejce (VEY-tseh)
Soup	Polévka (poh-LEHV-kah)
Dessert	Dezert (DEH-zehrt)

Write the right words down twice on the next page

Cheese ....

Meat ....

Dessert ....

Vegetables ....

Fruit ....

Milk ....

Vegetables ....

Eggs ....

Soup ....

Dessert ....

Bread ....

Rice ....

Meat ....

Fruit ....

Milk ....

Cheese ....

Bread ....

Eggs ....

Soup ....

Rice ....

Week 1

Day 5: Animals

Dog	Pes (pehs)
Cat	Kočka (KOH-chkah)
Lion	Lev (lehv)
Sheep	Ovce (OHV-tseh)
Pig	Prase (PRAH-seh)
Monkey	Opice (OH-pee-tseh)
Tiger	Tygr (TEE-grr)
Bear	Medvěd (MEHD-vyehd)
Horse	Kůň (koonz)
Bird	Pták (ptaak)

Write the right words down twice on the next page

Monkey	....	....
Cat	....	....
Bird	....	....
Lion	....	....
Sheep	....	....
Pig	....	....
Monkey	....	....
Tiger	....	....
Bear	....	....
Horse	....	....
Bird	....	....
Dog	....	....
Cat	....	....
Lion	....	....
Sheep	....	....
Pig	....	....
Horse	....	....
Tiger	....	....
Bear	....	....
Dog	....	....

Week 1

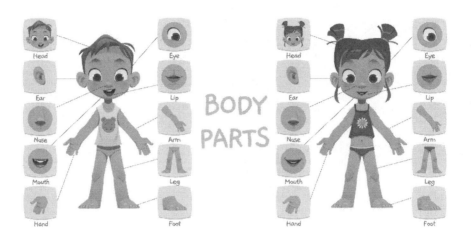

Day 6: Body

Head	Hlava (HLAH-vah)
Neck	Krk (krk)
Belly	Břicho (BRZHEE-khoh)
Shoulder	Rameno (RAH-meh-noh)
Knee	Koleno (koh-LEH-noh)
Back	Záda (ZAH-dah)
Arms	Ruce (ROO-tseh)
Hands	Ruce (ROO-tseh)
Legs	Nohy (NOH-hee)
Feet	Nohy (NOH-hee)

Write the right words down twice on the next page

Shoulder	....	....
Back	....	....
Feet	....	....
Belly	....	....
Hands	....	....
Shoulder	....	....
Knee	....	....
Back	....	....
Arms	....	....
Hands	....	....
Neck	....	....
Feet	....	....
Head	....	....
Neck	....	....
Belly	....	....
Knee	....	....
Legs	....	....
Arms	....	....
Head	....	....
Legs	....	....

Week 1

Day 7: Weather

Sun	Slunce (SLUHN-tseh)
Rain	Déšť (DYEH-sht')
Cloud	Oblak (OH-blahk)
Wind	Vítr (VEE-tr)
Snow	Sníh (snee)
Thunder	Hrom (hrom)
Lightning	Blesk (blesk)
Storm	Bouře (BOH-rzhe)
Fog	Mlha (ML'ha)
Rainbow	Duha (DOO-ha)

Write the right words down twice on the next page

Storm	....	....
Rain	....	....
Fog	....	....
Snow	....	....
Cloud	....	....
Wind	....	....
Snow	....	....
Thunder	....	....
Rain	....	....
Lightning	....	....
Storm	....	....
Fog	....	....
Rainbow	....	....
Sun	....	....
Cloud	....	....
Wind	....	....
Thunder	....	....
Lightning	....	....
Rainbow	....	....
Sun	....	....

Week 2

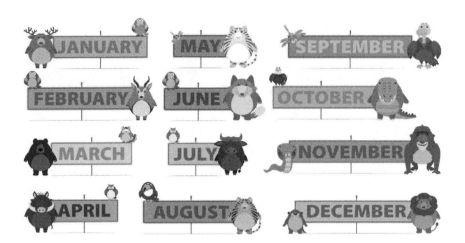

Day 8: Months

January	Leden (LEH-den)
February	Únor (OON-or)
March	Březen (BRZHEH-zen)
April	Duben (DOO-ben)
May	Květen (KVYEH-ten)
June	Červen (CHER-ven)
July	Červenec (CHER-veh-nets)
August	Srpen (SR'pen)
September	Září (ZAH-zhee)
October	Říjen (RZHEE-yen)

Write the right words down twice on the next page

October ....

February ....

August ....

October ....

April ....

May ....

June ....

August ....

March ....

September ....

May ....

January ....

July ....

March ....

April ....

June ....

January ....

July ....

February ....

September ....

Week 2

Day 9: School

Teacher	Učitel (OO-chee-tel)
Student	Student (STOO-dent)
Classroom	Třída (TRZHEE-dah)
Book	Kniha (KNEE-hah)
Pen	Pero (PEH-ro)
Pencil	Tužka (TOOZH-kah)
Desk	Psací stůl (PSAH-tsee stool)
Chair	Židle (ZHEE-dleh)
Homework	Domácí úkol (DOH-mah-tsee OO-kohl)
Exam	Zkouška (ZKOH-shkah)

Write the right words down twice on the next page

Chair	....	....
Homework	....	....
Teacher	....	....
Student	....	....
Classroom	....	....
Exam	....	....
Pen	....	....
Pencil	....	....
Desk	....	....
Classroom	....	....
Homework	....	....
Exam	....	....
Teacher	....	....
Student	....	....
Desk	....	....
Book	....	....
Pen	....	....
Pencil	....	....
Chair	....	....
Book	....	....

Week 2

Day 10: Transportation

Car	Auto (OW-toh)
Bus	Autobus (OW-toh-boos)
Train	Vlak (vlahk)
Bicycle	Bicykl (BEE-tsee-kl)
Motorcycle	Motocykl (MOH-toh-tsee-kl)
Boat	Lod' (lodh)
Airplane	Letadlo (LEH-tahd-loh)
Helicopter	Vrtulník (VRT-ool-neek)
Truck	Náklad'ák (NAHK-lah-dzhaak)
Metro	Metro (MEH-troh)

Write the right words down twice on the next page

Airplane	....	....
Bus	....	....
Train	....	....
Metro	....	....
Truck	....	....
Motorcycle	....	....
Boat	....	....
Airplane	....	....
Helicopter	....	....
Truck	....	....
Metro	....	....
Car	....	....
Bus	....	....
Train	....	....
Bicycle	....	....
Helicopter	....	....
Motorcycle	....	....
Boat	....	....
Bicycle	....	....
Car	....	....

Week 2

Day 11: Clothing

Shirt	Košile (KOH-shee-leh)
Pants	Kalhoty (KAL-ho-tee)
Dress	Sukně (SOOK-nyeh)
Skirt	Sako (SAH-koh)
Jacket	Boty (BOH-tee)
Shoes	Ponožky (POH-nozh-kee)
Socks	Klobouk (KLOH-bouk)
Hat	Rukavice
Gloves	(ROO-kah-vee-tseh)
Scarf	Šátek (SHA-tehk)

Write the right words down twice on the next page

Socks	....	....
Pants	....	....
Dress	....	....
Jacket	....	....
Skirt	....	....
Scarf	....	....
Shoes	....	....
Socks	....	....
Hat	....	....
Gloves	....	....
Scarf	....	....
Shirt	....	....
Pants	....	....
Dress	....	....
Skirt	....	....
Jacket	....	....
Shoes	....	....
Gloves	....	....
Hat	....	....
Shirt	....	....

Week 2

Day 12: Emotions

Happy	Šťastný (SHTAH-stnee)
Sad	Smutný (SMOOT-nee)
Angry	Naštvaný (NAHS-tvah-nee)
Excited	Vzrušený (VZROO-sheh-nee)
Surprised	Překvapený (PRZHEHK-vah-peh-nee)
Scared	Vyděšený (VEE-dyeh-sheh-nee)
Nervous	Nervózní (NER-vohz-nee)
Bored	Nudný (NOOD-nee)
Confused	Zmatený (ZMAH-teh-nee)
Calm	Klidný (KLID-nee)

Write the right words down twice on the next page

Confused   ....

Happy   ....

Calm   ....

Surprised   ....

Sad   ....

Angry   ....

Excited   ....

Nervous   ....

Scared   ....

Nervous   ....

Bored   ....

Scared   ....

Calm   ....

Happy   ....

Sad   ....

Bored   ....

Angry   ....

Excited   ....

Surprised   ....

Confused   ....

Week 2

Day 13: Hobbies

Reading	Čtení (CHTEH-nee)
Painting	Malování (MAH-loh-vah-nee)
Singing	Zpěv (ZPEHV)
Dancing	Tanec (TAH-nets)
Cooking	Vaření (VAH-rzheh-nee)
Photography	Fotografie (FOH-toh-grah-fee-eh)
Sleeping	Spaní (SPA-nee)
Writing	Psaní (PSAH-nee)
Gardening	Zahradničení (ZAH-hrad-nee-cheh-nee)
Sports	Sport (spohrt)

Write the right words down twice on the next page

Gardening	....	....
Painting	....	....
Photography	....	....
Painting	....	....
Dancing	....	....
Cooking	....	....
Photography	....	....
Sports	....	....
Writing	....	....
Gardening	....	....
Sports	....	....
Reading	....	....
Sleeping	....	....
Singing	....	....
Dancing	....	....
Cooking	....	....
Singing	....	....
Sleeping	....	....
Writing	....	....
Reading	....	....

Week 2

Day 14: Sports

Football	Fotbal (FOHT-bahl)
Basketball	Basketbal (BAHS-keht-bahl)
Tennis	Tenis (TEH-nees)
Swimming	Plavání (PLAH-vah-nee)
Volleyball	Volejbal (VOH-lei-bahl)
Golf	Golf (golf)
Cycling	Cyklistika (TSIHK-lees-tee-kah)
Running	Běh (byeh)
Fitness	Fitness (FIT-ness)
Martial arts	Bojová umění (BOH-yoh-vah OO-meh-nee)

Write the right words down twice on the next page

Swimming	....	....
Football	....	....
Fitness	....	....
Basketball	....	....
Golf	....	....
Swimming	....	....
Volleyball	....	....
Golf	....	....
Running	....	....
Cycling	....	....
Running	....	....
Fitness	....	....
Martial arts	....	....
Football	....	....
Basketball	....	....
Tennis	....	....
Martial arts	....	....
Volleyball	....	....
Cycling	....	....
Tennis	....	....

Week 3

Day 15: Nature

Tree	Strom (strohm)
Flower	Květina (KVYEH-tee-nah)
River	Řeka (RZHEH-kah)
Mountain	Hora (HOH-rah)
Lake	Jezero (YEZ-eh-roh)
Beach	Pláž (plahzh)
Forest	Les (lehss)
Grass	Tráva (TRAH-vah)
Star	Hvězda (HVYEHZ-dah)
Cloud	Oblak (OH-blahk)

Write the right words down twice on the next page

Grass	....	....
Beach	....	....
Mountain	....	....
Cloud	....	....
Flower	....	....
River	....	....
Mountain	....	....
Lake	....	....
Beach	....	....
Forest	....	....
Grass	....	....
Star	....	....
Forest	....	....
Cloud	....	....
Tree	....	....
Flower	....	....
River	....	....
Star	....	....
Lake	....	....
Tree	....	....

Week 3

Day 16: Days of the Week

Monday	Pondělí (POHN-dye-lee)
Tuesday	Úterý (OO-teh-ree)
Wednesday	Středa (STRZHEH-dah)
Thursday	Čtvrtek (CHTVUR-tek)
Friday	Pátek (PAH-tek)
Saturday	Sobota (SOH-boh-tah)
Sunday	Neděle (NEH-dye-leh)
Yesterday	Včera (VCHER-ah)
Tomorrow	Zítra (ZEE-trah)
Today	Dnes (dnehss)

Write the right words down twice on the next page

Sunday	....	....
Tuesday	....	....
Saturday	....	....
Today	....	....
Wednesday	....	....
Tomorrow	....	....
Friday	....	....
Saturday	....	....
Yesterday	....	....
Tomorrow	....	....
Today	....	....
Monday	....	....
Thursday	....	....
Wednesday	....	....
Thursday	....	....
Friday	....	....
Monday	....	....
Sunday	....	....
Yesterday	....	....
Tuesday	....	....

Week 3

Day 17: Music

Song	Píseň (PEE-sehn)
Melody	Melodie (MEH-loh-dyeh)
Rhythm	Rytmus (RIHT-moos)
Instrument	Nástroj (NAHS-troy)
Singing	Zpěv (ZPEHV)
Band	Kapela (KAH-peh-lah)
Concert	Koncert (KON-tsert)
Piano	Klávesy (KLAH-veh-seh)
Guitar	Kytara (KI-tah-rah)
Sound	Zvuk (zvook)

Write the right words down twice on the next page

Concert	....	....
Melody	....	....
Rhythm	....	....
Sound	....	....
Guitar	....	....
Piano	....	....
Instrument	....	....
Singing	....	....
Band	....	....
Piano	....	....
Guitar	....	....
Sound	....	....
Song	....	....
Rhythm	....	....
Instrument	....	....
Singing	....	....
Band	....	....
Concert	....	....
Song	....	....
Melody	....	....

Week 3

Day 18: Jobs

Teacher	Učitel (OO-chee-tel)
Doctor	Lékař (LEH-karzh)
Engineer	Inženýr (IN-zheh-neer)
Chef	Šéfkuchař (SHEHF-koo-khahr)
Police officer	Policista (POH-lee-tsee-stah)
Firefighter	Hasič (HAH-seech)
Nurse	Sestra (SEHS-trah)
Pilot	Pilot (PEE-loht)
Lawyer	Právník (PRAHV-neek)
Artist	Umělec (OO-meh-lets)

Write the right words down twice on the next page

Lawyer	....	....
Teacher	....	....
Chef	....	....
Doctor	....	....
Engineer	....	....
Chef	....	....
Police officer	....	....
Pilot	....	....
Nurse	....	....
Doctor	....	....
Artist	....	....
Teacher	....	....
Pilot	....	....
Engineer	....	....
Artist	....	....
Police officer	....	....
Firefighter	....	....
Nurse	....	....
Lawyer	....	....
Firefighter	....	....

Week 3

Day 19: Fruits

Apple	Jablko (YAH-buhl-koh)
Banana	Banán (BAH-nahn)
Orange	Pomeranč (POH-meh-rahnch)
Strawberry	Jahoda (YAH-hoh-dah)
Grapes	Hrozny (HROZ-nee)
Watermelon	Meloun (MEH-loh-oon)
Pineapple	Ananas (AH-nah-nahss)
Mango	Mango (MAHN-goh)
Kiwi	Kivi (KEE-vee)
Peach	Broskev (BROHS-kehv)

Write the right words down twice on the next page

Orange	....	....
Apple	....	....
Banana	....	....
Orange	....	....
Mango	....	....
Grapes	....	....
Kiwi	....	....
Pineapple	....	....
Mango	....	....
Peach	....	....
Apple	....	....
Banana	....	....
Strawberry	....	....
Grapes	....	....
Watermelon	....	....
Pineapple	....	....
Kiwi	....	....
Strawberry	....	....
Peach	....	....
Watermelon	....	....

Week 3

Day 20: Vegetables

Carrot	Mrkev (MR-kehv)
Tomato	Rajče (RAI-cheh)
Potato	Brambora (BRAHM-boh-rah)
Onion	Cibule (TSIH-boo-leh)
Cucumber	Okurka (OH-koor-kah)
Broccoli	Brokolice (BROH-koh-lee-tseh)
Spinach	Špenát (SHPEH-naht)
Corn	Kukuřice (KOO-koo-rzhits-eh)
Cabbage	Zelí (ZEHL-ee)
Mushroom	Houba (HOH-bah)

Write the right words down twice on the next page

Corn ....

Tomato ....

Potato ....

Mushroom ....

Spinach ....

Onion ....

Broccoli ....

Spinach ....

Corn ....

Tomato ....

Mushroom ....

Carrot ....

Cucumber ....

Potato ....

Onion ....

Cucumber ....

Cabbage ....

Carrot ....

Cabbage ....

Broccoli ....

Week 3

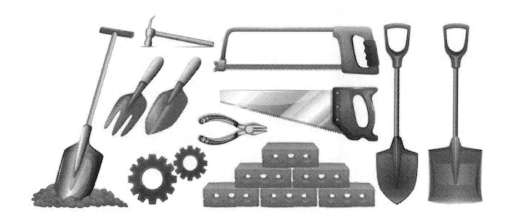

Day 21: Tools

Hammer	Kladivo (KLAH-dee-voh)
Screwdriver	Šroubovák (SHROO-boh-vahk)
Wrench	Klíč (kleech)
Pliers	Kombinéza (kohm-bin-AY-zah)
Saw	Pila (PEE-lah)
Drill	Vrták (VRT-ahk)
Tape measure	Měřicí páska (MYESH-ee-tsee PAHS-kah)
Chisel	Dláto (DLAH-toh)
Level	Lopata (LOH-pah-tah)
Paintbrush	Štětka (SHTYET-kah)

Write the right words down twice on the next page

Level	....	....
Screwdriver	....	....
Wrench	....	....
Paintbrush	....	....
Pliers	....	....
Drill	....	....
Chisel	....	....
Level	....	....
Paintbrush	....	....
Hammer	....	....
Screwdriver	....	....
Pliers	....	....
Saw	....	....
Drill	....	....
Tape measure	....	....
Hammer	....	....
Wrench	....	....
Saw	....	....
Chisel	....	....
Tape measure	....	....

Week 4

Day 22: Kitchen

Plate	Talíř (TAH-leerzh)
Fork	Vidlička (VID-leech-kah)
Knife	Nůž (noozh)
Spoon	Lžíce (LZHEE-tseh)
Cup	Hrnek (HR-nehk)
Bowl	Miska (MEE-skah)
Pan	Pánev (PAH-nehv)
Pot	Hrnce (HRN-tseh)
Cutting board	Řezací prkno (RZEH-zah-tsee PRK-noh)
Oven	Trouba (TROH-bah)

Write the right words down twice on the next page

Plate	....	....
Oven	....	....
Fork	....	....
Bowl	....	....
Knife	....	....
Spoon	....	....
Cup	....	....
Cutting board	....	....
Knife	....	....
Fork	....	....
Bowl	....	....
Spoon	....	....
Pan	....	....
Pot	....	....
Cutting board	....	....
Oven	....	....
Pot	....	....
Plate	....	....
Cup	....	....
Pan	....	....

Week 4

Day 23: Instruments

Guitar	Kytara (KY-tah-rah)
Piano	Klávesy (KLAH-veh-seh)
Violin	Housle (HOH-sleh)
Flute	Flétna (FLEHT-nah)
Trumpet	Trubka (TRUHB-kah)
Drum	Bubny (BOOB-nee)
Saxophone	Saxofon (SAK-soh-fohn)
Cello	Violoncello (vee-oh-lon-TSEL-loh)
Clarinet	Klarinet (KLAR-ee-net)
Harp	Harfa (HAR-fah)

Write the right words down twice on the next page

Flute	....	....
Piano	....	....
Trumpet	....	....
Violin	....	....
Cello	....	....
Trumpet	....	....
Drum	....	....
Saxophone	....	....
Cello	....	....
Clarinet	....	....
Violin	....	....
Saxophone	....	....
Harp	....	....
Guitar	....	....
Drum	....	....
Piano	....	....
Harp	....	....
Flute	....	....
Guitar	....	....
Clarinet	....	....

Week 4

Day 24: Buildings

House	Dům (doom)
School	Škola (SHKO-lah)
Hospital	Nemocnice (NEH-mots-nee-tseh)
Library	Knihovna (KNEE-hov-nah)
Bank	Banka (BAHN-kah)
Restaurant	Restaurace (RES-tau-raht-seh)
Hotel	Hotel (hoh-TEL)
Museum	Muzeum (moo-ZEH-oom)
Church	Kostel (KOS-tel)
Stadium	Stadion (STAH-dyon)

Write the right words down twice on the next page

Hospital	....	....
House	....	....
Museum	....	....
School	....	....
Stadium	....	....
Hospital	....	....
Church	....	....
Restaurant	....	....
Hotel	....	....
Museum	....	....
Church	....	....
House	....	....
School	....	....
Library	....	....
Bank	....	....
Restaurant	....	....
Hotel	....	....
Library	....	....
Bank	....	....
Stadium	....	....

Week 4

Day 25: Directions

Left	Vlevo (VLEH-voh)
Right	Vpravo (VPRAH-voh)
Straight	Rovně (ROHV-nyeh)
Up	Nahoru (NAH-hoh-roo)
Down	Dolů (DOH-loo)
North	Sever (SEH-ver)
South	Jih (yih)
East	Východ (VEE-khod)
West	Západ (ZAH-pahd)
Stop	Stůj (stooi)

Write the right words down twice on the next page

Straight ....

Left ....

South ....

Straight ....

Up ....

Down ....

North ....

Stop ....

East ....

Stop ....

Left ....

Right ....

South ....

Right ....

North ....

West ....

Up ....

Down ....

East ....

West ....

Week 4

Day 26: Bedroom

Bed	Postel (POHS-tel)
Pillow	Polštář (POLSH-tarzh)
Blanket	Přikrývka (PREE-kreev-kah)
Wardrobe	Šatní skříň (SHAHT-nee skrzheen)
Nightstand	Noční stolek (NOCH-nee STOH-lek)
Lamp	Lampa (LAHM-pah)
Alarm clock	Budík (BOO-deek)
Dresser	Komoda (KOH-moh-dah)
Hanger	Věšák (VYESH-ahk)
Mirror	Zrcadlo (ZUR-tsah-dloh)

Write the right words down twice on the next page

Hanger	....	....
Pillow	....	....
Dresser	....	....
Wardrobe	....	....
Mirror	....	....
Nightstand	....	....
Lamp	....	....
Alarm clock	....	....
Dresser	....	....
Blanket	....	....
Hanger	....	....
Mirror	....	....
Wardrobe	....	....
Nightstand	....	....
Bed	....	....
Blanket	....	....
Lamp	....	....
Bed	....	....
Alarm clock	....	....
Pillow	....	....

Week 4

Day 27: Countries

United States	Spojené státy (SPOY-ye-neh STAHT-ee)
United Kingdom	Spojené království (SPOY-ye-neh KRAH-lohv-stvee)
Canada	Kanada (KAH-nah-dah)
Australia	Austrálie (OWS-trah-lee-eh)
Germany	Německo (NYEH-mets-koh)
France	Francie (FRAN-tsee-eh)
China	Čína (CHEE-nah)
Japan	Japonsko (YAH-pohn-skoh)
Brazil	Brazílie (BRAH-zee-lyeh)
India	Indie (IN-dyeh)

Write the right words down twice on the next page

China ....

United States ....

India ....

Canada ....

Australia ....

Brazil ....

China ....

Japan ....

Brazil ....

India ....

United States ....

Germany ....

Canada ....

Australia ....

Japan ....

United Kingdom ....

Germany ....

France ....

United Kingdom ....

France ....

Week 4

Day 28: Travel

Airport	Letiště (LEH-teesh-tcheh)
Passport	Pas (pahs)
Ticket	Letenka (LEH-ten-kah)
Suitcase	Kufr (KOO-fr)
Hotel	Hotel (hoh-TEL)
Sightseeing	Památky (PAH-mah-tee-kee)
Beach	Pláž (plahzh)
Adventure	Dobrodružství (doh-broh-droozh-stvee)
Map	Mapa (MAH-pah)
Tourist	Turista (too-REES-tah)

Write the right words down twice on the next page

Airport	....	....
Adventure	....	....
Passport	....	....
Ticket	....	....
Suitcase	....	....
Hotel	....	....
Sightseeing	....	....
Beach	....	....
Adventure	....	....
Map	....	....
Tourist	....	....
Airport	....	....
Passport	....	....
Ticket	....	....
Suitcase	....	....
Hotel	....	....
Sightseeing	....	....
Beach	....	....
Map	....	....
Tourist	....	....

Week 5

Day 29: Health

Doctor	Lékař (LEH-kahrzh)
Hospital	Nemocnice (neh-MOTS-neet-seh)
Medicine	Lék (lehk)
Nurse	Sestra (SEHS-trah)
Pain	Bolest (BOH-lest)
Appointment	Termín (TEHR-meen)
Exercise	Cvičení (tsvee-CHEH-nyee)
Sleep	Spánek (SPAH-nehk)
Diet	Strava (STRAH-vah)
Vitamin	Vitamín (vee-tah-MEEN)

Write the right words down twice on the next page

Appointment	....	....
Vitamin	....	....
Hospital	....	....
Medicine	....	....
Nurse	....	....
Pain	....	....
Sleep	....	....
Hospital	....	....
Exercise	....	....
Nurse	....	....
Sleep	....	....
Diet	....	....
Vitamin	....	....
Doctor	....	....
Pain	....	....
Appointment	....	....
Exercise	....	....
Doctor	....	....
Medicine	....	....
Diet	....	....

Week 5

Day 30: Languages

English	Angličtina (AHN-gleech-tee-nah)
Spanish	Španělština (shpah-NYELSH-tee-nah)
French	Francouzština (fran-TSOOZH-tee-nah)
German	Němčina (NYEM-chee-nah)
Dutch	Holandština (hoh-LAHND-shtee-nah)
Frisian	Fríština (FREE-shtee-nah)
Russian	Ruština (ROOSH-tee-nah)
Portuguese	Portugalština (por-too-GAHL-shtee-nah)
Japanese	Japonština (yah-POHN-shtee-nah)
Italian	Italština (ee-TAHL-shtee-nah)

Write the right words down twice on the next page

German ....

Spanish ....

Portuguese ....

French ....

German ....

Dutch ....

Frisian ....

Russian ....

Italian ....

Russian ....

Japanese ....

Frisian ....

English ....

Italian ....

English ....

Spanish ....

French ....

Dutch ....

Portuguese ....

Japanese ....

Week 5

Day 31: Church

Priest	Kněz (knyehz)
Worship	Bohoslužba (boh-hoh-SLOOZH-bah)
Prayer	Modlitba (MOHD-leet-bah)
Bible	Bible (BEE-bleh)
Sermon	Kázání (KAAH-zah-nyee)
Choir	Sbor (zbohr)
Altar	Oltář (ohl-TAHRZH)
Cross	Kříž (krzheezh)
Faith	Víra (VEE-rah)
Ceremony	Obřad (OHB-rzahd)

Write the right words down twice on the next page

Choir	....	....
Worship	....	....
Altar	....	....
Bible	....	....
Ceremony	....	....
Faith	....	....
Sermon	....	....
Choir	....	....
Altar	....	....
Cross	....	....
Faith	....	....
Ceremony	....	....
Cross	....	....
Priest	....	....
Worship	....	....
Prayer	....	....
Bible	....	....
Sermon	....	....
Priest	....	....
Prayer	....	....

Week 5

Day 32: Birds

Eagle	Orel (OH-rel)
Sparrow	Vrabec (VRAH-bets)
Owl	Sova (SOH-vah)
Parrot	Papoušek (PAH-poh-shek)
Hummingbird	Kolibřík (koh-LEE-bzheek)
Pigeon	Holub (HOH-loob)
Flamingo	Plameňák (PLAH-meh-nyahk)
Swan	Labuť (LAH-boot)
Peacock	Páv (PAHV)
Duck	Kachna (KAHKH-nah)

Write the right words down twice on the next page

Duck	....	....
Eagle	....	....
Sparrow	....	....
Owl	....	....
Eagle	....	....
Swan	....	....
Sparrow	....	....
Flamingo	....	....
Hummingbird	....	....
Pigeon	....	....
Flamingo	....	....
Owl	....	....
Swan	....	....
Peacock	....	....
Duck	....	....
Parrot	....	....
Hummingbird	....	....
Pigeon	....	....
Parrot	....	....
Peacock	....	....

Week 5

Day 33: Science

Chemistry	Chemie (KHEH-mee-yeh)
Biology	Biologie (bee-oh-LOH-gyeh)
Physics	Fyzika (FY-zee-kah)
Astronomy	Astronomie (ahs-troh-NOH-mee-yeh)
Experiment	Experiment (ehk-speh-REEM-ent)
Laboratory	Laboratoř (lah-boh-rah-TOHRZH)
Microscope	Mikroskop (MEE-kroh-skop)
Hypothesis	Hypotéza (hee-poh-TEH-zah)
Scientist	Vědec (VYEH-dets)
Discovery	Objev (OH-byev)

Write the right words down twice on the next page

Hypothesis	…………………..	…………………..
Biology	…………………..	…………………..
Experiment	…………………..	…………………..
Astronomy	…………………..	…………………..
Physics	…………………..	…………………..
Astronomy	…………………..	…………………..
Microscope	…………………..	…………………..
Scientist	…………………..	…………………..
Laboratory	…………………..	…………………..
Physics	…………………..	…………………..
Microscope	…………………..	…………………..
Hypothesis	…………………..	…………………..
Chemistry	…………………..	…………………..
Scientist	…………………..	…………………..
Discovery	…………………..	…………………..
Chemistry	…………………..	…………………..
Biology	…………………..	…………………..
Laboratory	…………………..	…………………..
Discovery	…………………..	…………………..
Experiment	…………………..	…………………..

Week 5

Day 34: Film

Actor	Herec (HEH-rets)
Actress	Herečka (HEH-rech-kah)
Director	Režisér (reh-ZHEE-sehr)
Script	Scénář (SCEH-nahrzh)
Camera	Kamera (KAH-meh-rah)
Scene	Scéna (SCEH-nah)
Drama	Drama (DRAH-mah)
Comedy	Komedie (KOH-meh-dyeh)
Action	Akce (AHK-tseh)
Television	Televize (teh-leh-VEE-zeh)

Write the right words down twice on the next page

Actor ....

Camera ....

Action ....

Director ....

Script ....

Television ....

Camera ....

Scene ....

Drama ....

Comedy ....

Action ....

Television ....

Actor ....

Actress ....

Director ....

Scene ....

Actress ....

Drama ....

Comedy ....

Script ....

Week 5

Day 35: History

Ancient	Starověký (stah-ROH-vyeh-kee)
Civilization	Civilizace (tsee-vee-lee-ZAH-tseh)
Emperor	Císař (CHEE-sahrzh)
Revolution	Revoluce (reh-voh-LOO-tseh)
War	Válka (VAHL-kah)
Kingdom	Království (KRAH-lohv-stvee)
Archaeology	Archeologie (ar-kheh-OH-loh-yeh)
Renaissance	Renesance (reh-neh-SAHN-tseh)
Independence	Nezávislost (neh-ZAH-vee-slost)
Event	Událost (OO-dah-lost)

Write the right words down twice on the next page

Kingdom ....

Event ....

Archaeology ....

Emperor ....

Renaissance ....

Independence ....

Revolution ....

War ....

Kingdom ....

Archaeology ....

Renaissance ....

Independence ....

Event ....

Ancient ....

Civilization ....

Emperor ....

Revolution ....

War ....

Ancient ....

Civilization ....

Week 6

Day 36: Drinks

Water	Voda (VOH-dah)
Coffee	Káva (KAAH-vah)
Tea	Čaj (chai)
Juice	Džus (joos)
Soda	Soda (SOH-dah)
Milk	Mléko (MLEH-koh)
Wine	Víno (VEE-noh)
Beer	Pivo (PEE-voh)
Cocktail	Koktejl (kohk-TAYL)
Lemonade	Limonáda (lee-moh-NAH-dah)

Write the right words down twice on the next page

Soda	....	....
Cocktail	....	....
Tea	....	....
Juice	....	....
Wine	....	....
Soda	....	....
Milk	....	....
Wine	....	....
Beer	....	....
Cocktail	....	....
Lemonade	....	....
Water	....	....
Coffee	....	....
Water	....	....
Tea	....	....
Lemonade	....	....
Juice	....	....
Milk	....	....
Coffee	....	....
Beer	....	....

Week 6

Day 37: Business

Entrepreneur	Podnikatel (pohd-nee-KAH-tel)
Company	Společnost (spoh-LECH-nost)
Marketing	Marketing (MAR-ke-ting)
Sales	Prodej (PROH-dey)
Product	Produkt (PROH-dukt)
Customer	Zákazník (ZAAH-kah-zneek)
Finance	Finance (FEE-nahn-tseh)
Strategy	Strategie (strah-TEH-gyeh)
Profit	Zisk (zeesk)
Investment	Investice (in-VEHS-tee-tseh)

Write the right words down twice on the next page

Strategy	....	....
Company	....	....
Marketing	....	....
Sales	....	....
Product	....	....
Customer	....	....
Finance	....	....
Investment	....	....
Customer	....	....
Profit	....	....
Finance	....	....
Investment	....	....
Entrepreneur	....	....
Company	....	....
Marketing	....	....
Sales	....	....
Product	....	....
Profit	....	....
Entrepreneur	....	....
Strategy	....	....

Week 6

Day 38: Beach

Sand	Písek (PEE-sek)
Waves	Vlny (VL-nih)
Sunscreen	Opalovací krém (oh-pah-LOH-vah-tsee krehm)
Swim	Plavání (plah-VAH-nyee)
Seashells	Mušle (MOOSH-leh)
Umbrella	Deštník (DESH-teen-eek)
Beach ball	Plážový míč (PLAA-zhoh-vee meech)
Sunbathing	Opalování (oh-pah-LOH-va-nyee)
Surfing	Surfování (soor-FOH-va-nyee)
Picnic	Piknik (PEEK-neek)

Write the right words down twice on the next page

Beach ball	....	....
Sunbathing	....	....
Waves	....	....
Sunscreen	....	....
Picnic	....	....
Swim	....	....
Umbrella	....	....
Beach ball	....	....
Picnic	....	....
Sand	....	....
Sunscreen	....	....
Swim	....	....
Seashells	....	....
Surfing	....	....
Waves	....	....
Umbrella	....	....
Seashells	....	....
Sunbathing	....	....
Surfing	....	....
Sand	....	....

Week 6

Day 39: Hospital

Doctor	Doktor (DOHK-tohr)
Nurse	Sestra (SEHS-trah)
Patient	Pacient (PAH-tsyent)
Emergency	Nouzový případ (NOH-zoh-vee PREE-pahd)
Surgery	Operace (oh-peh-RAH-tseh)
Appointment	Termín (TEHR-meen)
Stethoscope	Stetoskop (STEH-toh-skop)
X-ray	Rentgen (RENT-gen)
Medicine	Lék (lehk)
Recovery	Rekonvalescence (reh-kohn-vah-LEHS-ents-eh)

Write the right words down twice on the next page

Nurse ....

Doctor ....

Appointment ....

Stethoscope ....

Emergency ....

Recovery ....

Nurse ....

Patient ....

Emergency ....

Surgery ....

Appointment ....

Stethoscope ....

X-ray ....

Medicine ....

Recovery ....

Doctor ....

Surgery ....

Patient ....

X-ray ....

Medicine ....

Week 6

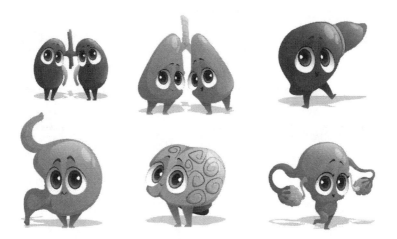

Day 40: Internal Body

Heart	Srdce (SIR-tseh)
Lungs	Plíce (PLEE-tseh)
Stomach	Žaludek (ZHAH-loo-dek)
Liver	Játra (YAAH-trah)
Kidneys	Ledviny (LEHD-vee-nee)
Brain	Mozek (MOH-zek)
Intestines	Střeva (STRZHEH-vah)
Bladder	Močový měchýř (MOH-tchoh-vee MEH-khyezh)
Bones	Kosti (KOH-stee)
Muscles	Svaly (SVAH-lee)

Write the right words down twice on the next page

Kidneys	....	....
Stomach	....	....
Heart	....	....
Intestines	....	....
Brain	....	....
Lungs	....	....
Stomach	....	....
Liver	....	....
Muscles	....	....
Kidneys	....	....
Intestines	....	....
Bladder	....	....
Bones	....	....
Muscles	....	....
Heart	....	....
Lungs	....	....
Bones	....	....
Liver	....	....
Brain	....	....
Bladder	....	....

Week 6

Day 41: Internet

Website	Webová stránka (VEH-boh-vah STRAAN-kah)
Email	Email (eh-MAYL)
Social media	Sociální média (soh-tsee-AHL-nee MAY-dee-ah)
Online shopping	Online nakupování (ON-line nah-koo-poh-VAH-nee)
Search engine	Vyhledávač (veeh-leh-DAH-vach)
Password	Heslo (HEHS-loh)
Wi-Fi	Wi-Fi (VEE-fee)
Download	Stáhnout (STAAH-noot)
Upload	Nahrát (NAH-raht)
Browser	Prohlížeč (proh-LEE-zhech)

Write the right words down twice on the next page

Browser	....	....
Website	....	....
Email	....	....
Social media	....	....
Wi-Fi	....	....
Search engine	....	....
Password	....	....
Wi-Fi	....	....
Download	....	....
Upload	....	....
Browser	....	....
Online shopping	....	....
Email	....	....
Social media	....	....
Online shopping	....	....
Password	....	....
Website	....	....
Download	....	....
Upload	....	....
Search engine	....	....

Week 6

Day 42: Shapes

Cirkel	Kruh (krooh)
Square	Čtverec (CHTVEH-rets)
Rectangle	Obdélník (ob-DYEH-leh-neek)
Triangle	Trojúhelník (troh-YOO-hehl-neek)
Oval	Ovál (oh-VAHL)
Pyramid	Pyramida (pee-RAH-mee-dah)
Cube	Krychle (KRIH-khleh)
Arrow	Šipka (SHEEP-kah)
Star	Hvězda (HVYEZ-dah)
Cylinder	Válec (VAH-lehts)

Write the right words down twice on the next page

Rectangle ....

Triangle ....

Pyramid ....

Arrow ....

Star ....

Cylinder ....

Oval ....

Square ....

Star ....

Cube ....

Cirkel ....

Pyramid ....

Cylinder ....

Cirkel ....

Square ....

Rectangle ....

Triangle ....

Oval ....

Cube ....

Arrow ....

Week 7

Day 43: House Parts

Roof	Střecha (STRZHEH-chah)
Door	Dveře (DVEH-zheh)
Window	Okno (OHK-noh)
Floor	Podlaha (poh-DAH-lah)
Wall	Stěna (STYEH-nah)
Ceiling	Strop (strop)
Stairs	Schody (SKHOH-dih)
Bathroom	Koupelna (KOH-pel-nah)
Kitchen	Kuchyně (KOO-khih-nyeh)
Bedroom	Ložnice (LOZH-nee-tseh)

Write the right words down twice on the next page

Wall	....	....
Door	....	....
Stairs	....	....
Ceiling	....	....
Floor	....	....
Wall	....	....
Ceiling	....	....
Bedroom	....	....
Stairs	....	....
Bathroom	....	....
Kitchen	....	....
Bedroom	....	....
Roof	....	....
Door	....	....
Window	....	....
Floor	....	....
Roof	....	....
Bathroom	....	....
Kitchen	....	....
Window	....	....

Week 7

Day 44: Around the House

Plant	Rostlina (ros-TLEE-nah)
Watering can	Konvice na zalévání (KON-vee-tseh nah ZAH-leh-vah-nee)
Shed	Zahradní domek (ZAH-rah-dnee DOH-mek)
Doorbell	Zvonek (ZVOH-nek)
Fence	Plot (plot)
Mailbox	Poštovní schránka (POHSH-tohv-nee SKHRRAHN-kah)
Lawn mower	Sekačka na trávu (SEH-kach-kah nah TRAH-voo)
Wheelbarrow	Kolečko (koh-LECH-koh)
Shovel	Lopata (LOH-pah-tah)
Bench	Lavička (LAH-veech-kah)

Write the right words down twice on the next page

Watering can	....	....
Shed	....	....
Doorbell	....	....
Mailbox	....	....
Bench	....	....
Fence	....	....
Wheelbarrow	....	....
Shed	....	....
Mailbox	....	....
Bench	....	....
Lawn mower	....	....
Wheelbarrow	....	....
Shovel	....	....
Plant	....	....
Watering can	....	....
Doorbell	....	....
Fence	....	....
Lawn mower	....	....
Shovel	....	....
Plant	....	....

Week 7

Day 45: Face

Eyes	Oči (OH-chee)
Nose	Nos (nohs)
Mouth	Ústa (OOS-tah)
Ears	Uši (OO-shee)
Cheeks	Tváře (TVAHR-zheh)
Forehead	Čelo (CHEH-loh)
Chin	Brada (BRAH-dah)
Lips	Rty (rtee)
Teeth	Zuby (ZOO-bee)
Eyebrows	Obočí (oh-BOH-chee)

Write the right words down twice on the next page

Eyebrows	....	....
Nose	....	....
Chin	....	....
Forehead	....	....
Ears	....	....
Cheeks	....	....
Forehead	....	....
Chin	....	....
Nose	....	....
Lips	....	....
Teeth	....	....
Eyebrows	....	....
Eyes	....	....
Lips	....	....
Teeth	....	....
Mouth	....	....
Ears	....	....
Mouth	....	....
Cheeks	....	....
Eyes	....	....

Week 7

Day 46: Bathroom

Sink	Dřez (drzehz)
Toilet	Záchod (ZAH-khod)
Shower	Sprcha (SPRH-chah)
Bathtub	Vana (VAH-nah)
Mirror	Zrcadlo (ZRCAH-dloh)
Towel	Ručník (ROOCH-neek)
Soap	Mýdlo (MEED-loh)
Toothbrush	Zubní kartáček (ZOOP-nee KAR-tah-chehk)
Shampoo	Šampon (SHAHM-pohn)
Hairdryer	Fén (fehn)

Write the right words down twice on the next page

Mirror	....	....
Sink	....	....
Hairdryer	....	....
Shower	....	....
Bathtub	....	....
Mirror	....	....
Towel	....	....
Soap	....	....
Toothbrush	....	....
Toilet	....	....
Shampoo	....	....
Towel	....	....
Soap	....	....
Hairdryer	....	....
Sink	....	....
Toilet	....	....
Shower	....	....
Bathtub	....	....
Toothbrush	....	....
Shampoo	....	....

Week 7

Day 47: Living Room

Sofa	Pohovka (POH-hov-kah)
Television	Televize (teh-leh-VEE-zeh)
Coffee table	Konferenční stolek (kon-feh-RENCH-nee STOH-lehk)
Bookshelf	Knižní police (KNEEZ-nee POH-lee-tseh)
Lamp	Lampa (LAHM-pah)
Rug	Koberec (koh-BEH-rets)
Cushion	Polštář (POHL-shtaarzh)
Remote control	Dálkový ovladač (DAHL-koh-vee ov-lah-DAHCH)
Curtains	Závěsy (ZAA-vehs-ee)
Fireplace	Krb (krb)

Write the right words down twice on the next page

Rug ....

Sofa ....

Remote control ....

Television ....

Coffee table ....

Bookshelf ....

Lamp ....

Cushion ....

Curtains ....

Fireplace ....

Sofa ....

Television ....

Fireplace ....

Lamp ....

Rug ....

Cushion ....

Remote control ....

Curtains ....

Bookshelf ....

Coffee table ....

Week 7

Day 48: Finance

Budget	Rozpočet (ROZ-poh-chet)
Savings	Úspory (OOS-por-ih)
Debt	Dluh (dlooh)
Income	Příjem (PRZHI-yehm)
Expenses	Výdaje (VEE-dah-yeh)
Bank account	Bankovní účet (BAHN-kov-nee OO-chet)
Credit card	Kreditní karta (KREH-deet-nee KAR-tah)
Interest	Úrok (OOR-ok)
Loan	Půjčka (POOYCH-kah)
Stock market	Burza (BOOR-zah)

Write the right words down twice on the next page

Savings	....	....
Loan	....	....
Debt	....	....
Income	....	....
Expenses	....	....
Budget	....	....
Income	....	....
Expenses	....	....
Interest	....	....
Loan	....	....
Stock market	....	....
Budget	....	....
Bank account	....	....
Credit card	....	....
Debt	....	....
Savings	....	....
Interest	....	....
Bank account	....	....
Credit card	....	....
Stock market	....	....

Week 7

Day 49: Books

Writer	Spisovatel (spee-soh-VAH-tel)
Page	Stránka (STRAHN-kah)
Table of Contents	Obsah (OB-sah)
Foreword	Předmluva (PRZHEHD-mloo-vah)
Introduction	Úvod (OO-vod)
Front cover	Přední obálka (PRZHEHD-nee oh-BAHL-kah)
Back cover	Zadní obálka (ZAH-dnee oh-BAHL-kah)
Text	Text (text)
Title	Název (NAH-zehv)
Picture	Obrázek (oh-BRAH-zek)

Write the right words down twice on the next page

Front cover ....

Table of Contents ....

Title ....

Picture ....

Introduction ....

Back cover ....

Page ....

Foreword ....

Title ....

Text ....

Back cover ....

Picture ....

Writer ....

Page ....

Table of Contents ....

Foreword ....

Introduction ....

Front cover ....

Writer ....

Text ....

Week 8

Day 50: Law

Witness	Svědek (SVEH-dek)
Justice	Spravedlnost (sprah-VEHD-nohst)
Judge	Soudce (SOUD-tseh)
Victim	Oběť (OH-byech)
Perpetrator	Pachatel (PAH-hah-tel)
Court	Soud (soud)
Evidence	Důkaz (DOO-kahs)
Lawyer	Advokát (ahd-VOH-kaht)
Crime	Zločin (ZLOH-cheen)
Government	Vláda (VLAH-dah)

Write the right words down twice on the next page

Perpetrator	....	....
Court	....	....
Justice	....	....
Evidence	....	....
Victim	....	....
Government	....	....
Judge	....	....
Victim	....	....
Perpetrator	....	....
Court	....	....
Evidence	....	....
Lawyer	....	....
Crime	....	....
Government	....	....
Witness	....	....
Justice	....	....
Crime	....	....
Judge	....	....
Witness	....	....
Lawyer	....	....

More words for you

Questions	Otázky	....	....
Answers	Odpovědi	....	....
Think	Myslet	....	....
Know	Vědět	....	....
Understand	Rozumět	....	....
Show	Ukázat	....	....
Feel	Cítit	....	....
Hear	Slyšet	....	....
Take	Vzít	....	....
Give	Dát	....	....
Book	Kniha	....	....
Chair	Židle	....	....
Table	Stůl	....	....
Telephone	Telefon	....	....
Computer	Počítač	....	....
Game	Hra	....	....
Mountain	Hora	....	....
Forest	Les	....	....
River	Řeka	....	....
City	Město	....	....
Country	Země	....	....
Sea	Moře	....	....

Sun	Slunce	....	....
Moon	Měsíc	....	....
Man	Muž	....	....
Woman	Žena	....	....
Child	Dítě	....	....
Family	Rodina	....	....
Friend	Přítel	....	....
House	Dům	....	....
Car	Auto	....	....
Work	Práce	....	....
School	Škola	....	....
University	Univerzita	....	....
Eat	Jíst	....	....
Drink	Pít	....	....
Beer	Pivo	....	....
Wine	Víno	....	....
Cheese	Sýr	....	....
Big	Velký	....	....
Small	Malý	....	....
Good	Dobrý	....	....
Bad	Špatný	....	....
Young	Mladý	....	....
Old	Starý	....	....

Beautiful	Krásný	....	....
Ugly	Ošklivý	....	....
New	Nový	....	....
Fast	Rychlý	....	....
Slow	Pomalý	....	....
Warm	Teplý	....	....
Cold	Studený	....	....
Friendly	Přátelský	....	....
Unfriendly	Nepřátelský	....	....
Easy	Snadný	....	....
Heavy	Těžký	....	....
Expensive	Drahý	....	....
Cheap	Levný	....	....
Quiet	Tichý	....	....
Be	Být	....	....
Have	Mít	....	....
Do	Dělat	....	....
Go	Jít	....	....
Come	Přijít	....	....
See	Vidět	....	....
Hear	Slyšet	....	....
Speak	Mluvit	....	....
Read	Číst	....	....

Write	Psát	....	....
Eat	Jíst	....	....
Drink	Pít	....	....
Run	Běhat	....	....
Sleep	Spát	....	....
Work	Pracovat	....	....
Learn	Učit se	....	....
Help	Pomáhat	....	....
Play	Hrát	....	....
Search	Hledat	....	....
Buy	Koupit	....	....
Stay	Zůstat	....	....
Stand	Stát	....	....
Sit	Sedět	....	....
Carry	Nosit	....	....
Meet	Setkat	....	....
Leave	Odejít	....	....
Begin	Začít	....	....
Tell	Vyprávět	....	....
Win	Vyhrát	....	....
Lose	Prohrát	....	....
Open	Otevřít	....	....
Close	Zavřít	....	....

English	Czech		
Improve	Zlepšit	....	....
Explain	Vysvětlit	....	....
Follow	Následovat	....	....
Remember	Pamatovat	....	....
Forget	Zapomenout	....	....
Pay	Platit	....	....
Sell	Prodat	....	....
Send	Poslat	....	....
Receive	Přijmout	....	....
Decide	Rozhodnout	....	....
Visit	Navštívit	....	....
Love	Milovat	....	....
Hate	Nenávidět	....	....
Celebrate	Slavit	....	....
Dance	Tančit	....	....
Sing	Zpívat	....	....
Jump	Skočit	....	....
Newspaper	Noviny	....	....
Magazine	Časopis	....	....
Letter	Dopis	....	....
Card	Karta	....	....
Gift	Dárek	....	....
Party	Párty	....	....

English	Czech		
Holidays	Dovolená	....	....
Travel	Cestovat	....	....
Photo	Fotografie	....	....
Camera	Fotoaparát	....	....
Light	Světlo	....	....
Art	Umění	....	....
Culture	Kultura	....	....
History	Historie	....	....
Nature	Příroda	....	....
Environment	Životní prostředí	....	....
Weather	Počasí	....	....
Rain	Déšť	....	....
Snow	Sníh	....	....
Ice	Led	....	....
Fast	Rychlý	....	....
Slow	Pomalý	....	....
Early	Brzy	....	....
Late	Pozdě	....	....
Simple	Jednoduchý	....	....
Difficult	Složitý	....	....
Strong	Silný	....	....
Weak	Slabý	....	....
Correct	Správný	....	....

Wrong	Špatný	....	....
Safe	Bezpečný	....	....
Dangerous	Nebezpečný	....	....
Important	Důležitý	....	....
Interesting	Zajímavý	....	....
Boring	Nudný	....	....
Happy	Šťastný	....	....
Sad	Smutný	....	....
Healthy	Zdravý	....	....
Sick	Nemocný	....	....
Tired	Unavený	....	....
Animal	Zvíře	....	....
Dog	Pes	....	....
Cat	Kočka	....	....
Bird	Pták	....	....
Fish	Ryba	....	....
Horse	Kůň	....	....
Street	Ulice	....	....
Way	Cesta	....	....
Bridge	Most	....	....
Square	Náměstí	....	....

Help Us Share Your Thoughts!

Dear reader,

We hope you enjoyed reading this book as much as we enjoyed making it for you. This book is part of a special collection from **Skriuwer (www.skriuwer.com)**, a global community dedicated to creating books that make language learning an engaging and enjoyable experience.

Our journey doesn't end here. We believe that every reader is part of our growing family. If there was anything in this book you did not like, or if you have suggestions for improvement, we are all ears! Do not hesitate to contact us at **kontakt@skriuwer.com**. Your feedback is extremely valuable in making our books even better.

If you enjoyed your experience, we would be thrilled to hear about it! Consider leaving a review on the website where you purchased this book. Your positive reviews not only warm our hearts, but also help other language learners to discover and enjoy our books.

Thank you very much for choosing **Skriuwer**. Let's continue to explore the wonders of languages and the joy of learning together.

Warm regards,
The Skriuwer Team

Made in the USA
Las Vegas, NV
20 October 2024